An opinionated guide to

DESIGN LONDON

AF077464

Written by
SUJATA BURMAN
AND ROSA BERTOLI

Design Museum (no.40)

INFORMATION IS DEAD. LONG LIVE OPINION.

Good design comes in many forms. What delights one person might fall flat for the next.

The point of these guide books is not to try and please all people but, like truly good design, to provide just enough structure and stimulus to create a worthwhile, useful experience.

So here you have it: an unashamedly opinionated guide to the best design in London, whether that be architecture, shops, galleries or restaurants. We've intentionally made a tight edit of our favourites, so that what remains is the best of the best. If you want to find endless information, go online. If you want short and sweet opinion, read on.

Martin
Hoxton Mini Press

Present & Correct (no.1)
Opposite: Vitra (no.10)

St Giles Square (no.13)
Opposite: Another Country (no.58)

CONTRIBUTORS

Sujata Burman is a writer, editor and lifelong Londoner. She has worked with global design and culture publications and institutions, and held roles at *Wallpaper** magazine, London Design Festival and London Design Biennale. In work and life, Sujata is always seeking to make the fields of design and architecture accessible and joyful to wider audiences.

Rosa Bertoli was born in Udine, Italy, and now lives in London. As the Global Design Director of *Wallpaper** magazine, she has written extensively about all areas of design, moderated design talks and conferences in London and abroad and has been on several judging panels. She is interested in uncovering the ways in which design and everyday life inform and impact each other.

Riya Patel is an editor, writer and proud south Londoner who's travelled the world reporting on the latest products and furniture for design magazines including *Icon*, *Frame* and *Wallpaper** magazine. The best bits of her job are nosing around designers' studios and spotting the next generation of talent at graduate shows.

FOREWORD

The best bit of design to come out of London might be something people don't consider design at all – the tube map. Initially rejected by London's transport officials for being 'too radical', draughtsman Harry Beck's 1933 map eventually triumphed, mercifully untangling the city's mass of stations, streets, alleyways and endless quirks into a foolproof legend of standard lines, colours and symbols. Copied the world over, its unrivalled efficiency showed how best to zip along subterranean routes, saving tired legs and valuable minutes for urban exploration.

It was the first and only piece of design I could get my hands on as a teenager, looking at London from the suburbs with a sense of awe. In the age before smartphones, my dog-eared pocket A–Z was always at the ready, smoothing the way for first visits to many of the temples of design you'll find in these pages. First came the formidable brick-and-stone maze of South Kensington's V&A Museum (no.36), brimming with examples of Britain's Victorian-era design and manufacturing prowess, all neatly categorised into rooms of delicate glass, looping ironwork, ornate wood carvings and stern-faced busts.

Later, I ventured to Covent Garden and the famous store of Zeev Aram (no.7), where I'd eventually work as curator of the in-house gallery. Aram was among the first to bring modern furniture and lighting from Italy to London in the

1960s. In a country more used to chintz, doilies and reproduction antiques, people were entirely unprepared for gleaming chrome, bent plywood and black leather – legend has it someone hated the furniture so much they threw a brick through the shop window. These days, they're the revered trailblazers to whom we owe much of the furniture populating our homes – from glass side tables and tripod plant holders to brass pendant lights and modular sofas.

Where Milan is a slick showcase of Italy's major manufacturing clout and Stockholm epitomises the serene Scandinavian aesthetic, London is a young and rebellious design capital that makes its own rules, reinventing itself yearly as new shops, galleries, restaurants and neighbourhoods join the scene. When some disappear, as is sadly frequent in a city with sky-high rents, I'm always cheered to see a plucky newcomer step up and move in with a fresh idea or novel take.

A lot of this reinvention comes about through sheer personal willpower, a drive that has led the most wonderfully individual and borderline eccentric labours of love. The meticulously organised stationery mecca of Present & Correct (no.1) is one such undertaking. Rows of ring-bound notebooks, little glass bowls of shiny brass tacks and paperclips in unusual shapes, sharp pencils and vintage finds are the perfect tonic for the chaos of the city outside.

In central and west London, rising design stars are presented in galleries that exist in the orbit of larger museums and institutions, while east London is flavoured by its industrial past as the seat of the city's furniture industry. Shoreditch is home to Jasper Morrison (no.21), the secretive product designer known for his pure functional forms, and retailer SCP (no.2), with a foothold since 1985 and a mission to promote British designers with rotating exhibitions in its huge warehouse premises on Curtain Road.

Today, the most exciting developments are happening in the north and south. In King's Cross, the snaking re-development of Coal Drops Yard is home to the studio and store of rockstar-turned-industrial-designer Tom Dixon (no.14). South of the river, the makers at Cockpit Arts Deptford (no.34) have revitalised the former 1960s council office they call home with funding from the London Mayor. The makeshift workshops now sit around a courtyard garden full of wild plants and a public cafe, plus leather and woodworking facilities, to preserve this unique creek-side community space.

Finally, some of the best design in London is public: free for everyone to enjoy, just like Beck's map. Take Yinka Ilori's flamingo-themed playground (no.19), inspired by joyful memories of his childhood estate, or the handmade ceramic tube station mosaic at Seven Sisters by Assemble and Matthew Raw (no.17). London owes a lot to its designers, makers and inventors. This excellent guide will let you in on a few more stories of the risk-takers and revolutionaries that have shaped the city.

Riya Patel
London, 2024

BEST FOR...

Galleries and museums

Expand your design education at these storied London institutions that bring the art of making to the fore. Start with the V&A (no.36), whose galleries offer a historical overview of creativity across centuries and geographies, then move on to the nearby Design Museum (no.40) for a contemporary (and often pop culture-led) take on the subject. A more everyday side of design can be explored at the Museum of the Home (no.22) or the Young V&A (no.18), both excellent examples of how design plays a vital role in everyday life.

Shopping

These days, (good) design is more accessible than ever, and you can swing by several London establishments to bring a piece home with you. Step into Japan House (no.46) for some of the most desirable objects and craft, or browse beautiful stationery at Present & Correct (no.1). Labour and Wait (no.25) and the Jasper Morrison shop (no.21) offer the most practical design in the city, while Liberty (no.48) and Paul Smith (no.54) are the destinations of choice for unique gifts, from exclusive fragrances to elegant fabrics.

Eating and drinking
A good meal or pint can be kicked up a notch by being taken in stylish surroundings. Lucky that in London, we're spoiled for choice. Enter striking tile heaven at The Standard hotel bar (no.6) or immerse yourself in Bauhaus at A Bar with Shapes for a Name (no.20). For artfully dressed spaces, stick to The Audley (no.52) or the aesthetically pleasing tearoom and Instagram-friendly toilets at sketch (no.39).

Window shopping
Who doesn't like to fantasise about their ideal home? You'll find plenty of opportunities to indulge in house inspo at Aram (no.7) with an expansive gallery spaces chock-full of decades of design classics. Alternatively, try out the furniture at SCP (no.2). For serious renovation motivation, explore iyouall (no.30) and twentytwentyone (no.15).

Design in public space
Getting around London can be stressful, so we appreciate design moments across the city that offer some respite. Take your pick from the mosaics at Tottenham Court Road (no.12), the swivelling marble public seating at St Giles Square (no.13) or game stations on a busy high street in Bexleyheath (no.35).

SEASONAL EVENTS

CLERKENWELL DESIGN WEEK
Held in one of the most densely populated areas for design and architectural practices in Europe, CDW might be geared towards industry types, but there's also plenty of talks, launches and aperitivos along the trail that bring in a wider audience.
May / clerkenwelldesignweek.com

LONDON CRAFT WEEK
Every May, guests from 40 countries join with galleries, brands, shops and even cafes to celebrate creativity and making. Explore demonstrations of craft from weaving to pottery, millinery to embroidery, and exhibitions of artisan-made objects.
May / londoncraftweek.com

LONDON FESTIVAL OF ARCHITECTURE
Debating ideas around architecture, celebrating emerging talent and exploring new ways of designing cities – this festival hosts interactive pop-ups across town to raise awareness of the critical importance of design and research to urban planning.
June / londonfestivalofarchitecture.org

NEW DESIGNERS
See London's rising stars under one roof, with the latest and greatest work from graduates in all areas of design – from graphics and industrial design to furniture and textiles.
June–July / newdesigners.com

LONDON DESIGN BIENNALE

This design takeover fills Somerset House with country 'pavilions' responding to themes in design innovation. The neoclassical surrounds are the ideal backdrop for this family-friendly affair, when the courtyard and terrace might turn into an immersive forest, maze or Indian city chowk.

June / londondesignbiennale.com

LONDON DESIGN FESTIVAL

LDF is a design-led city takeover. Within numerous 'districts' or mini design hubs, 300 events take place, from artist open studios, talks on AI and mixed reality installations. Best of all, most of it is free.

September / londondesignfestival.com

OPEN HOUSE FESTIVAL

For a few days in September, almost every architecturally significant private home or inaccessible institution is open to the public. Explore a rich variety of private homes, embassies, religious buildings, studios and workshops.

September / programme.openhouse.org.uk

PAD

Since 2007, a huge black tent in Berkeley Square has been erected yearly to host some of the most elite galleries in a design, jewellery, art and craft extravaganza. Enter the dimly lit tent to discover a plethora of beautiful objects in an intimate setting.

October / padesignart.com

CENTRAL

1
PRESENT & CORRECT
Beautiful stationery you never knew you needed

Every stationery need is delightfully catered for by Present & Correct, who operate out of a minimalist and pristine plywood space in Bloomsbury, just steps away from the British Museum. A one-stop-shop for all things paper, pencils and more, inside you'll discover a curated selection of vintage and contemporary writing tools and accessories covering everyday essentials, iconic calendars, desk organisers and a few select oddities (think graph paper-patterned socks and faux crayon flasks). Inspired by museum displays and designed to mimic the intricate arrangements that characterised Renaissance curiosity cabinets, the shop's delightfully spare interior is part of the charm, its arrangement made flexible and modular to suit its evolving retail needs.

12 Bury Place, WC1A 2JL
Nearest station: Holborn
presentandcorrect.com

2
SCP

The East End's original design shop

Home renovators with a discerning eye should make their way to SCP, named after British design advocate and owner Sheridan Coakley. Everything inside its two storeys is handpicked by Coakley, with stylish furniture and products that are both manufactured in-house and by global design brands. Sofas, lighting and outdoor furniture are invitingly arranged to ressemble rooms in a trendy home. For thirsty browsers, there's even a branded coffee shop on the ground floor. SCP's connection with the city's design scene is even more apparent during London Design Festival, as it is the heart (and founder) of the Shoreditch Design Triangle, a network of cultural activities in this East End zone.

135–139 Curtain Road, EC2A 3BX
Nearest station: Shoreditch High Street
scp.co.uk

CENTRAL

3
SOMERSET HOUSE

An evolving forum for culture

The courtyard at Somerset House is imbued with a shape-shifting power: one minute it's a spellbinding festive ice rink, and the next a sun-drenched playground for children to splash around in water fountains, or hosting open-air live music beneath the stars. The harmoniously proportioned neoclassical landmark is central to London's cultural life, and bursting at the seams with innovative artist studios, exhibitions, restaurants and cafes – and of course, historic art institution the Courtauld Gallery. Its events calendar is well worth tracking, but design lovers should absolutely visit during the London Design Biennale for global pavilions within the historic walls, or Collect Art Fair to ogle (or buy) crafty works.

Strand, WC2R 1LA
Nearest station: Temple
somersethouse.org.uk

CENTRAL

4
VIADUCT

A warehouse for interior inspiration

Leave behind the comparatively sleepy Clerkenwell surroundings and enter into an array of busy vignettes comprised of furniture, lighting and more. Global brands from Anglepoise to Knoll sit side by side with products by renowned designers like Naoto Fukasawa and Hans Wegner. The adaptable space is geared towards interior designers and architects looking to fill a client's home or fit out a new hotel or retail space, but the mezzanine attracts all sorts during Clerkenwell Design Week, with curated shows offering thematic displays or highlighting new launches from hot contemporary design brands like Flos, Please Wait To Be Seated and Vitra (no.10).

1–10 Summers Street, EC1R 5BD
Nearest station: Farringdon
viaduct.co.uk

CENTRAL

5
TOKYOBIKE

Minimalist cool on two wheels

More than just bikes, this compact shop just off Old Street is an ode to functional design objects that are also incredibly desirable. Their iconic bikes, first conceived in Tokyo in 2002, have light and practical frames for a smooth urban ride where every element is carefully considered, right down to the delicious colour palettes of elegant neutral hues and design-led shades of bright red, olive green, mustard yellow and pale blue. If cycling isn't your thing, their minimalist shop also sells an array of covetable Japanese items, from sleek kitchen utensils and gardening tools to desktop accessories. Don't miss their exhibitions, highlighting work from independent artists whose illustrations embody the utilitarian spirit and pleasing aesthetic of the space.

87–89 Tabernacle Street, EC2A 4BA
Nearest station: Old Street
tokyobike.co.uk

CENTRAL

6
THE STANDARD, LONDON

A paradise for colourful tile art

Don't be put off by the slightly intimidating Brutalist exterior of this hotel, which in a former life was Camden's town hall. Step inside, and it's quite a different story – a whirlwind of colour. Multi-hued tile art decorates the ground floor at the Double Standard bar, the basement bathroom and Library, where you can kick back, have a drink and read up on anything from chaos to religion. If you're checking in for the night, the tiled heaven continues, but in various forms: some rooms incorporate a nautical theme, while others, for those with deeper pockets, throw in an outdoor hot tub.

10 Argyle Street, WC1H 8EG
Nearest station: King's Cross St Pancras
standardhotels.com

CENTRAL

7
ARAM STORE

Design mastery in action

The four floors of modern design in this family-run, light-drenched industrial warehouse on Drury Lane practically constitute a design museum – full as it is with hidden gems and remarkable discoveries. Trail the red stairs to find icons and special editions by some of the most famous designers and brands of the 20th century, from Eames to Eileen Gray, Italian masters to Scandinavian minimalists. Despite all this hefty prestige, Aram doesn't get too bogged down in the past, and its exhibitions often showcase contemporary, emerging work from the likes of students and graduates from the Material Futures Masters course at Central Saint Martins.

110 Drury Lane, WC2B 5SG
Nearest station: Covent Garden
aram.co.uk

CENTRAL

8
LEE BROOM SHOWROOM

The city's resident wizard of light

Furniture and lighting designer Lee Broom emerged on the London scene in 2007 with a background in fashion, bringing all the drama of his previous career with him. The Shoreditch location is set in a network of design hotspots (SCP and Vitra are just a few streets down – see no.2 and no.10), but Broom's space shines bright, with imaginative designs and installations showing how creative you can really go with lighting. Make a beeline for the space during London Design Festival, when it transforms into a kaleidoscope of illuminating ideas, from carousels to a Roman-inspired domus, bringing every lamp to life in a theatrical and emotional setting.

93 Rivington Street, EC2A 3AY
Nearest station: Shoreditch High Street
leebroom.com

CENTRAL

9
MAGCULTURE

A haven for magazine junkies

If you love print, you'll likely have heard of mag-Culture. A passion project dreamt up by creative director Jeremy Leslie, the space was initially set up as a design studio but expanded to champion magazines from around the globe, with over 700 different publications available in the Clerkenwell store. While we're all tapping away on our phones and beset by screens, surfing the shelves at magCulture and seeing how people continue to innovate in the world of print grants a blissful hiatus. If you don't make it to the shop, keep an eye out for their pop-ups at design events across the city.

70 St John Street, EC1V 4PE
Nearest station: Angel
magculture.com

CENTRAL

10
VITRA TRAMSHED

Design takeover in the Tramway

Set in a 1905 electricity transformer station for the Eastern London Tramway, Londoners might remember Vitra's Shoreditch showroom as the location for Tramshed, Mark Hix's restaurant whose main feature was a giant cow by Damien Hirst that dominated the dining room. The vibe has shifted, as the space was reworked by the German furniture manufacturer to bring about a massive (but respectful) transformation of the heritage building in 2022. And with it, they've brought in an array of colourful furniture and objects by some of the world's leading designers. Needless to say, design is king here, with the main space dedicated to the brand's eclectic offering and temporary displays in the basement gallery that explore Vitra's history with legendary pieces from past and present.

32 Rivington Street, EC2A 3LX
Nearest station: Old Street
vitra.com

11
MAGMA

More than just a brilliant bookshop

Sitting on the less manic side of Covent Garden, Magma's central London space is filled with gems for design lovers. In addition to its sizeable magazine offering, the space is brimming with giftable design for any age – there are enigmatic games like Monkey Bingo right the way through to a stuffed, grinning Totoro from the beloved Miyazaki film, while the 'Make your own Mondrian' puzzle will propel your kids onto their art and design journey early. If it so happens that you *are* here to leaf through the magazines, make your way downstairs to experience the full gamut of niche titles available, including our favourite, *Catnip*, a magazine for lovers of cats and cat culture.

29 Short's Gardens, WC2H 9AP
Nearest station: Covent Garden
Other location: Clerkenwell
magma-shop.com

CENTRAL

12
TOTTENHAM COURT ROAD STATION

Pop Art mosaics amid commuter chaos

The London underground might seem monotonous, but a pit stop at Tottenham Court Road station could well change your mind. A series of mosaics created in the 1980s by artist Eduardo Paolozzi adorn some of the station's platforms and corridors, bringing to life the artist's visual universe using forms mixed with anthropomorphic characters, abstract figures and machinery components. While not all mosaics remained in situ after construction work in 2017 to link the station with the Elizabeth line, many were restored and remain part of the Tottenham Court Road experience. Upstairs by the ticket office, a new artwork by French artist Daniel Buren echoes Paolozzi's pieces: a series of colourful geometries welcoming commuters into the station.

Oxford Street, WC1A 1DG

CENTRAL

13
ST GILES SQUARE

A playground of seating

When designer Sabine Marcelis was invited to 'activate' St Giles Square for London Design Festival 2022, she took it as an opportunity to bring colour, geometry and movement into the space. Commissioned as a temporary project and then kept as part of the square's public furniture, her installation was conceived as a 'playground of seating'. Sit and swivel on one of the ten marble chairs, whose shapes are a nod to the architecture of Centre Point, the Brutalist icon that towers over the square. Made of stacked geometric forms in contrasting colourful stones, the mix of travertine, quartzite and marble comes in shades of green, red, yellow, blue and purple, their surfaces defined by speckles, lines and other graphic textures.

St Giles Square, WC2H 8AP
Nearest station: Tottenham Court Road

14
COAL OFFICE

Tom Dixon's creative laboratory

British designer Tom Dixon lived many creative lives before becoming one of the country's most celebrated designers. After spending the first half of the 1970s as a bass guitarist, Dixon began welding makeshift furniture pieces and selling them as quickly as he could make them. Visitors to the King's Cross superstore can experience his wildly successful global brand offering in the form of furniture, lighting, accessories and home fragrances (among which, 'Earth' is an irresistible blend of mint, guaiac wood and cedar). His canalside HQ also houses a showroom for Italian furniture company Porro and plentiful pop-up exhibitions from among the star-studded galaxy of Dixon's design friends – Coal Office is also a key central hub during London Design Festival.

2 Bagley Walk, N1C 4PQ
Nearest station: King's Cross
tomdixon.net

NORTH

15
TWENTYTWENTYONE

Dangerously desirable homeware

It's hard to walk past this iconic shop without taking a peek inside but, be warned: to do so will inevitably lead to a full-blown expedition. Exquisite wooden toys by Danese, Penco Sellotape dispensers, smart Tiipoi tea towels and the occasional Noguchi lamp will be hard to pass by and you'll leave with your pockets lighter and your bags heavier. With helpful descriptions of each brand and production methods, even design newbies aren't safe. True to its name, this store celebrates 20th- and 21st-century design – those looking for more of a deep dive into key design moments from this era should make a beeline for the Clerkenwell showroom during London Design Festival for its curated exhibitions.

274–275 Upper Street, N1 2UA
Nearest station: Highbury & Islington
Other location: Clerkenwell
twentytwentyone.com

16
ISOKON GALLERY

London's modernist moment

Nestled within leafy Hampstead, this charming gallery celebrates the modernist building it is set within – the iconic Isokon Flats. Small but smart, the gallery opened in 2014 in what was originally the Grade I-listed building's garage. Go to learn about the pioneering history of Isokon and its famous inhabitants, including Agatha Christie, designer Marcel Breuer and Walter Gropius of Bauhaus fame. If you're a real design aficionado, there's the added treat of Isokon's rotating exhibitions, which are inspired by the Bauhaus movement and the building's history.

Lawn Road, NW3 2XD
Nearest station: Belsize Park
isokongallery.org

NORTH

17
CLAY STATION

Craft and coffee

Commissioned in 2017 as part of Transport for London's Art on the Underground cultural programme, this humble retail space by Seven Sisters station was reinvented by Turner-prize winning artistic collective Assemble in collaboration with ceramicist Matthew Raw. The team wanted to elevate the formerly abandoned space to make an impact on the station and local experience. The design pays homage to the London underground's tiling heritage and, by installing an on-site kiln for the duration of the project they were able to make over 1,000 unique tiles and create a masterpiece of ceramic cladding in blue and canary yellow that now happens to serve equally invigorating coffee.

665 Seven Sisters Road, N15 5LA
Nearest station: Seven Sisters

18
YOUNG V&A

A history of toys

The Young V&A, rebranded from 'The Museum of Childhood' in 2023 after a three-year renovation, was the year's most highly anticipated reopening for those with kids in tow. While retaining many of the original displays, including Rachel Whiteread's beautiful 'Place (Village)' which consists of over 100 dollhouses, and cabinets of toys from every century guaranteed to bring multi-generation nostalgia, there is much more to discover. Beyond the expanded exhibition space is a new theatre, a floor of interactive games ranging from a safe-to-roam toddler space, to building blocks and an open studio for craft and making. Generating mixed reactions – those who liked it better before, those who prefer its new guise and the rare undecided – it's an undeniably exciting comeback for London's museum scene.

Cambridge Heath Road, E2 9PA
Nearest station: Bethnal Green
vam.ac.uk

19
FLAMBOYANCE OF FLAMINGOS

Bold, colourful play

Old-school London wasn't all smog-stained buses and pinstripe suits; in the 1970s, Barking residents may remember how Parsloes Park was a seasonal home to flocks of flamingos. This surreal bit of local history is the inspiration behind Yinka Ilori's bold playground that brings back the birds in highly stylised form, as fuchsia and bubblegum-pink curvilinear seating, bouncy spring rockers and a roundabout – all gloriously flamingo-themed. It's a perfect reflection of Ilori's work, where vibrant design is joined with a socially conscious approach. A much-loved fixture across the city, his large-scale motivational slogans have been seen from Canary Wharf to London Bridge, rendered in bright, juicy colours with a distinctive visual aesthetic inspired by his own Nigerian heritage.

Ivy Walk, RM9 5RX
Nearest station: Becontree

20

A BAR WITH SHAPES FOR A NAME

Drinking den for design geeks

Have you got a soft spot for Bauhaus? Then head straight to this enigmatically named bar-cum-laboratory to drink in the primary colours and shapes that pepper the space. Circle, triangle and square-shaped ice cubes match the geometric theme. The journey begins as you're greeted by a staff member dressed in a joyfully colourful jumpsuit, before taking a seat in one of the minimalist Muller Van Severen chairs in the 'school room' area, where herbs and spices hang from the ceiling. In essence, the bar enthusiastically channels the spirit of experimentation that fuelled the Bauhaus movement itself back in 1919.

232 Kingsland Road, Whitmore Estate, E2 8AX
Nearest station: Haggerston
instagram.com/@a_bar_with_shapes_for_a_name

21
JASPER MORRISON SHOP

A modern twist on classic homeware

British designer Jasper Morrison describes his shop as 'a modern interpretation of the classic hardware store'. Occupying a small space beside his east London studio, Morrison offers a selection of anonymous objects chosen as much for their functionality as for their aesthetic, which mirrors his own no-nonsense, practical designs – many of which are on sale alongside the selection. Go for hand-carved wooden spoons, classic espresso makers and furniture designed by Morrison for the likes of Vitra (no.10). Otherwise, visit during the London Design Festival, when the shop doubles as a gallery hosting temporary exhibitions that bring insight into the designer's universe and creative community.

24b Kingsland Road, E2 8DA
Nearest stations: Hoxton, Old Street
jaspermorrisonshop.com

EAST

22
MUSEUM OF THE HOME
The many meanings of home

What does home mean to you? Visitors are greeted with this question on entering a series of rooms that explore the many meanings of domestic life and how people inhabit spaces. Occupying a series of 300-year-old almshouses in Hoxton built to home pensioners, the museum uses objects, experiences and spaces to unpack what makes a home. The focus is on people and the individual approach to interiors, no matter how humble, with displays that explore religious rituals, technology and care. Upstairs, meanwhile, is a more traditional museum showing interiors from the 17th century onwards, with engaging captions bringing visitors into residents' stories, from the experiences of young caregivers to considering how displayed objects express cultural identity.

136 Kingsland Road, E2 8EA
Nearest station: Hoxton
museumofthehome.org.uk

23
ÆLFRED

Covert cache of budget-friendly Scandi chic

London modernist design aficionados have been blessed by dealer Nina Hertig's expert curatorial eye since 2005, when her gallery Sigmar opened on King's Road to showcase marvellous mid-century and contemporary pieces. The 2022 opening of her Hackney Wick warehouse shop Ælfred has been welcomed with equal enthusiasm. A decidedly different offering to Hertig's elevated west London enterprise. Here Scandinavian furniture spans desirable classics to more obscure artworks and objects, from Alvar Aalto tables to mismatched crockery, with prices ranging from £15 to £2,500.

Unit 2, Autumn Yard, Autumn Street, E3 2TT
Nearest station: Bow Road
aelfred.co.uk

24
THE MARKSMAN

The design-led pub

No ordinary pub, the Marksman's unassuming exterior conceals an upstairs dining room filled with marquetry tables, a whimsically upholstered ceiling, diamond-patterned Linoleum flooring and colourful chairs. Brightening up any lunchtime celebration, Italian artist Martino Gamper's design brings a playful touch to the dog-friendly local. Its stylish upgrade from Victorian pub to exuberantly design-led restaurant came in 2015, from which point the pub has played host to a knowingly hip crowd to match and earned a Michelin star for its smart cuisine.

254 Hackney Road, E2 7SB
Nearest stations: Hoxton, Bethnal Green
marksmanpublichouse.com

25
LABOUR AND WAIT

Elevating the ordinary

When Labour and Wait opened in east London, it was a big deal. The name was a nod to Henry Wadsworth Longfellow's exhortation to 'Learn to labour and to wait'; the year was 2000, and no other place better turned the everyday into the intensely desirable like this one-room wonder. Overnight, enamel plates, itchy sailor jumpers and traditional wooden brooms became must-haves, as the shop propelled everyone to recognise the beauty and potential of timeless classics. Many retailers have since followed suit, but Labour and Wait has kept its place in Londoners' hearts, with branches popping up in Marylebone as well as Dover Street Market – there's now even a Tokyo outpost.

85 Redchurch Street, E2 7DJ
Nearest station: Shoreditch High Street
Other location: Marylebone
labourandwait.co.uk

26
WILLIAM MORRIS GALLERY

Celebrating England's creative genius

You might not know the name, but chances are you've already seen William Morris's work: the Arts and Crafts textile designer, poet, artist, writer and activist created some of the most memorable fabric designs of the 20th century, with geometric repetitions of exquisite flora and fauna motifs featuring leaves and birds – the designs even appear on the local football team's kits. His family home in Walthamstow honours his work with displays of his wallpapers, textiles, tapestries and graphic design, and exhibitions spotlighting global craft and design that echo Morris's ethos of craft-based production. Make a day of it, and don't miss the extensive gardens surrounding the museum, with a garden trail that notes the plants used by Morris across his work.

Lloyd Park, Forest Road, E17 4PP
Nearest station: Walthamstow Central
wmgallery.org.uk

EAST

27
THE LINE

The city's free art trail

Are you a fan of Tracey Emin? Or Anthony Gormley? You can find works from these artists and others by walking the length of Stratford to Greenwich. Over 20 artworks are to be found integrated into the riverside landscape featuring glass towers, high-rise developments and, usually, ongoing construction. There's Helen Cammock's signage of small but powerful words emblazoned onto a bridge on Bow Creek, and a playful slide at the Olympic Park by Anish Kapoor and Carsten Höller. Bring a picnic and make your way through the trail on a sunny day, keeping an eye out for murals, sculptures and flags on this constantly evolving side of London.

Queen Elizabeth Park, E20 2A
Nearest station: Stratford
the-line.org

28
BRUNSWICK HOUSE

Grade II-listed antiques-packed mansion

Have you ever eaten a three-course meal, then left with the furniture you were seated on? No? Well, you haven't yet been to Brunswick House. Chef Jackson Boxer serves up some of London's hottest plates in this Georgian Palladian setting, where every vintage piece, opulent chandelier and even the occasional grandfather clock are up for grabs. Built for the Duke of Brunswick in 1758, the house later became a club for railway workers. Insider tip: make sure to time your visit for an intimate jazz night in the cellar.

30 Wandsworth Road, SW8 2LG
Nearest station: Vauxhall
brunswickhouse.london

SOUTH

29
THE KILN ROOMS

Ceramic-making for the soul

London may be swarming with pottery courses, but for community spirit The Kiln Rooms in Peckham is unbeatable. In their shop/gallery/teaching space you'll learn how to make your next favourite bowl, mug or vase, whether you're an aspiring potter or developing your throwing skills. The Kiln Rooms also frequently host shows, talks and workshops in their various open-access studios across Peckham, and one in Farringdon. Seek out one of the spaces nestled within Peckham's Copeland Park complex, which is itself a buzzing creative quarter packed with artist studios, pop-ups and a rooftop cinema during the summer months.

Unit 3, Copeland Park, 133 Rye Lane, SE15 3SN
Nearest station: Peckham Rye
Other location: Farringdon
thekilnrooms.com

SOUTH

30
IYOUALL

Giftable design in south London

Get your hands on gifts, accessories and even cosmetics from Scandinavian darlings like Hay, Ferm Living and Muuto in this curated design store that specialises in minimalist wares. Set up by IYA Studio, iyouall sits on the border of Peckham and East Dulwich, and its alluring shop front with furniture spilling out past the door will entice even the most jaded design devotees to pick up some wonderful new lighting and rugs to brighten the home. If it's bigger ticket items you're after, don't forget to take a peek downstairs where you might bag a Normann Copenhagen sofa or table.

48 East Dulwich Road, SE22 9AX
Nearest station: Peckham Rye
iyouall.com

31
STUDIO VOLTAIRE

Hotbed of experimental art, food and community

Art and design are embedded into the experience at Studio Voltaire. What used to be a Victorian mission hall aiding neighbouring Clapham Methodist Church is now its own temple to creativity, complete with a chapel-like facade. Depart the bustling streets of Clapham as you enter a tranquil, wild courtyard garden with homegrown fruit and veg, centring around a petite, cauliflower-shaped fountain and amber tiles glazed with volcanic ash. Once inside, you can enjoy lunch or a glass of artisanal wine at Crispin, surrounded by generous exhibition spaces and studios. Don't leave without visiting the playfully designed tiled toilet, a multi-hued art commission by Joanne Tatham and Tom O'Sullivan called, *The Institute For The Magical Effect Of Actually Giving A Shit (a note to our future self)*.

1a Nelsons Row, SW4 7JR
Nearest station: Clapham Common
studiovoltaire.org

SOUTH

32
FASHION AND TEXTILE MUSEUM

Craft and creativity in fashion

Despite being the country's only museum dedicated solely to fashion, this institution sits on the fringes of the industry. Founded by the iconic Dame Zandra Rhodes, the museum is now run by Newham College, one of the country's largest further education institutions, carrying out its original calling and mission to celebrate textiles, fashion, craft and creativity. Walking down Bermondsey Street, you can't miss its bold orange-and-bright-pink facade (the building is by Mexican architect Ricardo Legorreta, known for his lively colours and structured motifs). Inside, its exhibitions are dedicated to some of the most captivating creators in fashion and beyond, from Biba to Andy Warhol, and on key creative moments and movements from the history of textile design.

83 Bermondsey Street, SE1 3XF
Nearest station: London Bridge
fashiontextilemuseum.org

SOUTH

33
DESIGN DISTRICT

A playground of architectural styles

Yes, there actually *is* a 'Design District' in London, but conversely the main draw is the contemporary architecture. Each of the 16 buildings are dressed in expressive materials – you'll find surfaces made of Corten steel, or built from an iridescent metal that glimmers in the light with multi-hued reflections. Many of these are only accessible to those working within them or attending events, but you can stop for a bite to eat in the tree-lined Canteen building set inside a see-through bubble structure. If a trip out to Greenwich requires more activities to make it worthwhile, book a slot in London's first rooftop basketball court, or visit an exhibition at NOW Gallery, which is free to the public.

13 Soames Walk, SE10 0AX
Nearest station: North Greenwich
designdistrict.co.uk

34
COCKPIT

A haven of London makers

Cockpit started life as space for unemployed makers in 1986, and is now a go-to studios, housing around 150 independent creatives. An abundance of craft takes place across its two sites – one in Bloomsbury and one in Deptford – from 3D wax-printed jewellery-making and casting to ceramics inspired by fungi. The studios open twice a year, when visitors can get behind the scenes and meet the makers themselves, but the craft garden and cafe are inviting year-round. Fun fact: the Bloomsbury space is the reason for its name – it was originally an 18th-century cockfighting arena.

18–22 Creekside, SE8 3DZ
Nearest stations: Greenwich, Deptford
Other location: Bloomsbury
cockpitstudios.org

35
BEXLEYHEATH HIGH STREETS FOR ALL

Community-driven design

Public seating and signs are hardly ever well designed, but over in Bexleyheath they are levelling up. Furniture doubles as a games table in bright yellow and blue, and flags highlight some of the famous locals hailing from this southeast London spot, from Kate Bush to David Haye. Architect collective POoR worked with the community to capture the identities and cultures that make up this area, with design interventions that seek to fulfil and tap into societal needs. Bexleyheath High Streets for All brings a little fun to what usually is a concrete and shopfront-heavy high street, allowing people to come together to play, gossip or simply chill out.

Bexleyheath
Various locations
poorcollective.com

36
V & A

An emporium of creativity

Dubbed a 'schoolroom for everyone' by its first director, the prestigious V&A Museum holds some of the most dynamic collections of art and design from across Asia to Africa and through its diaspora communities – one minute you could be immersed in the tapestry galleries, and the next surrounded by glistening, sacred silver. This is also a mega hub of research and experimentation, with courses, talks and social events taking place beneath the grand Rotunda Chandelier in the main entrance as part of its 'Friday Late' series. Sunny days are best enjoyed in the John Madejski Garden and courtyard, a serene spot ideal for refreshments and admiring the building.

Cromwell Road, SW7 2RL
Nearest station: South Kensington
vam.ac.uk

37
CUBITTS BELGRAVIA

Spectacular spectacles in a timeless townhouse

Emerging design practice Child Studio have been quietly making a refined mark on select establishments across the city. One of our favourites is the Cubitts Belgravia shop, set within a 19th-century townhouse and imagined as a neoclassical drawing room updated with contemporary flair, defined by pale yellow walls that enhance the original plasterwork, mouldings and fireplace. The studio created distinctive bespoke panels to display specs and sunglasses, enriching the interiors with sophisticated mid-century furniture to create an intimate vibe. If you come for the interior design, stay to peruse their collections of timeless frames, or make your own from over 130 colours on offer.

43 Elizabeth Street, SW1W 9PP
Nearest station: Victoria
Other locations: Spitalfields,
Borough, Soho and elsewhere
cubitts.com

38
CROMWELL PLACE

Townhouses-turned-cultural hub

Beautiful design is no longer the preserve of white showcase rooms, and Cromwell Place, a creative space set across five townhouses in South Kensington, is the perfect antidote to that clinical aesthetic. Just like getting a tour through someone's home, the exhibitions naturally unfurl on each floor of the domestic setting, allowing for gentle discovery and moments where you're caught off guard by spiralling staircases and radiant natural light sifting through large windows set in frescoed ceilings. The cafe presents its own sanctuary, with plenty of 20th-century design classics to pair with your coup of bubbles.

4 Cromwell Place, SW7 2JE
Nearest station: South Kensington
cromwellplace.com

/ 39

SKETCH

Kaleidoscopic art and design

Snapping a picture in the Instagram-ready bathrooms at sketch is a rite of passage. The restaurant's surreal Pod Loos, set under a brightly chequered ceiling, will transport you to the 1960s set of *Austin Powers* – but sketch is so much more than that. Over its illustrious 20+ years of business, some of the greatest artists and designers have left their mark. Most famously, The Gallery dining room's interiors were created by French-Lebanese designer India Mahdavi and started life as a Shrigley-dedicated bubblegum-pink wonderland, before being reimagined in sunshine-yellow in collaboration with Yinka Shonibare in 2022.

9 Conduit Street, W1S 2XG
Nearest station: Oxford Circus
sketch.london

WEST

40
DESIGN MUSEUM

London's design landmark

A hop, skip and jump from its original location in Shad Thames, in 2016 the Design Museum reopened inside the 1960s building that formerly housed the Commonwealth Institute. Its mezzanine spaces are crawling with exhibitions in unusual spots, and the concept of design is unpacked in all its many shapes and sizes, with shows exploring anything from Barbie to Stanley Kubrick, Amy Winehouse to saris. Accessibility has been a key consideration here, as a way to engage those outside the industry, with the two design shops and permanent exhibition 'Designer Maker User' especially geared to learning.

224–238 Kensington High Street, W8 6AG
Nearest station: High Street Kensington
designmuseum.org

41
THE CONRAN SHOP

London's original tastemaker

Welcome to The Conran Shop's new era: a move from the legendary Michelin Building to a Sloane Square location as of September 2023. Inspired by Sir Terence Conran (the creative legend who dreamt up the destination in 1973 – and incidentally also founded the Design Museum [no.40]), the store reflects his vision for it to serve as 'a home of considered design and curated living'. Designed to look like a home itself, the shop features furniture, objects and home accessories that include the brand's own TCS Studio creations. And don't miss the shop's toilets, designed by Pentagram partner Sascha Lobe and inspired by French architect Le Corbusier's Modulor Man.

16 Sloane Square, SW1W 8ER
Nearest station: Sloane Square
theconranshop.com

42
GALLERY FUMI

A treasure trove of independent design

Valerio Capo and Sam Pratt founded Gallery Fumi in 2008 with the mission of discovering, promoting and celebrating the most exciting emerging designers in London and beyond. The gallery's offering has developed over the past 15 years, growing to include experimental craft, cutting edge furniture-making techniques and an energetic attitude towards creating. The offering now spans cardboard-box furniture and broken ceramics repaired kintsugi-style, marvellously complemented by glass chandeliers made to mimic long strands of spaghetti and colossal painted mirrors. In summary: don't come here for minimalism, forget functionality and embrace the unexpected.

2–3 Hay Hill, W1J 6AS
Nearest station: Green Park
galleryfumi.com

43
SOSHIRO

Diverse collaborations in an artist-led space

Cultural storytelling is at the heart of SoShiro gallery. Launched by Shiro Muchiri, an interior architect born in Kenya and trained in Milan, the Marylebone townhouse may seem like an uninviting private residence from the outside, but once you pass the door, it's all about inclusivity. The shows highlight the work of diverse artists from Ethiopia to Cuba, with a focus on artisans and women-led displays, and shoppable work dotted across the domestic setting. Time your visit for one of their events, when you might catch an inspiring talk on the power of culture in art and design, a wine and sake tastings or a pop-up exhibition of collectible design taking place during London Craft Week.

23 Welbeck Street, W1G 8DZ
Nearest station: Bond Street
soshiro.co

44
MODERNITY

Fine Nordic design in Pimlico

A Stockholm-based gallery specialising in Nordic mid-century design, Modernity opened its London outpost in 2023 and brought with it a plethora of well-considered products. Big-ticket names include the most legendary and coveted modernist gems, from Artek furniture by Alvar Aalto to Louis Poulsen lighting by Arne Jacobsen, but the gallery also offers more obscure furniture, ceramics and glassware. Modernity was the first tenant (and remains the highlight) of Newson's Yard on design dealer-heavy Pimlico Road. The former 1840 timber yard was carefully restored but retains its original red-brick features and atrium with skylights, making it an exciting discovery on a road that seemingly had no more secrets.

Newson's Yard, 57 Pimlico Road, SW1W 8NE
Nearest station: Sloane Square
modernity.se

45
SHREEJI NEWSAGENTS

Chic newsstand with global flair

Frontrunner for London's most picturesque newsagent, Shreeji is the real deal: inviting enough to feel like your average corner shop selling *Hello* magazine and Haribo sweets, it somehow also stocks the highest quality printed periodicals to be found in London today. Their eclectic stock ranges from cult design magazines like the Dutch *Capsule* to impossibly cool Japanese titles including *Casa Brutus* and *Popeye*, as well as go-to fashion mags from *Vogue* to *GQ*. There is much to discover in this design jewel of a shop, with plywood shelf-lined walls surrounding an onyx-topped desk. Stop by for coffee and cake or enjoy the shop's intimate back rooms by visiting during one of their many pop-ups, exhibitions or launches in collaboration with brands and magazines.

6 Chiltern Street, W1U 7PT
Nearest station: Bond Street
shreejinewsagents.com

46
JAPAN HOUSE LONDON

Japan's design on display

Diplomacy meets beauty in this sprawling celebration of Japan and everything that makes its culture so magnetic. The centre, led by the Government of Japan, opened in 2018 in an Art Deco building on Kensington High Street and hosts a shop, exhibition space and restaurant, all combining to offer a full Japanese experience. Start at the minimalist, meticulously laid out retail space, browsing from among the matcha-making essentials, printed scarves and tabi socks. Catch an exhibition downstairs, where astute programming provides an ongoing overview of design and craft in Japan, from silk braiding and woodworking to manga and dog architecture. End the visit with a trip to Akira restaurant and bar to dine while watching the chefs in action – if you're overwhelmed by choice, the bento box provides a delicious overview.

101–111 Kensington High Street, W8 5SA
Nearest station: High Street Kensington
japanhouselondon.uk

47
THE RIVER CAFE

A culinary institution

The connection between food and design may not be widely acknowledged, but The River Cafe's legendary status is one clear point of convergence. The pioneering restaurant that has birthed scores of celebrity chefs was originally a warehouse space that, in 1987, was transformed into a restaurant by Ruthie Rogers and became the stomping grounds for staff from her husband's office, architect Richard Rogers. Its sharp interiors have been renovated by the studio over the years, with highlights being the bright pink pizza oven and mirrored open kitchen. After your meal, swing by the River Cafe 'cafe' to get your hands on olive oil, cookware and the signature recipe book, all branded with the iconic kaleidoscopic bold graphic identity.

Thames Wharf, Rainville Road, W6 9HA
Nearest station: Hammersmith
rivercafe.co.uk

48
LIBERTY

Ultimate luxe design shopping

Luscious prints, Tudor revival and British luxury: Liberty is an icon of the London design scene. The building itself is an unmissable Regent Street landmark, constructed in the 1920s from decommissioned battleships. The dark wood-panelled interiors make the shopping experience feel singularly cosy, with each floor overlooking a central atrium frequently hosting inventive installations and pop-up collaborations. If six floors of painstakingly curated fashion, haberdashery, perfume labs and flower boutiques doesn't entice you, come back in winter for its lavish Christmas shop that leaves you no choice but to get into the festive spirit.

Regent Street, W1B 5AH
Nearest station: Oxford Circus
libertylondon.com

49
LADBROKE HALL

HQ of inventive design

A laboratory of experimentation for uber-luxury design and 'functional art', Ladbroke Hall plays HQ to Carpenters Workshop Gallery which also has outposts in Paris, New York and LA. Originally the Talbot Motor Company headquarters, the change of hands effectively transformed this 1903 Grade II-listed building into an arts club. The sprawling 43,000-square-foot location houses the gallery's exhibition space, an Italian restaurant headed up by chef Emanuele Pollini that delivers classics with a twist and film and video production studios, with an expanded cultural offering including Friday Jazz nights. Expect weird and wonderful design: cloud-like metal mesh chandeliers overlook perfectly preserved flowers trapped and suspended in resin objects, alongside abstract sculptural furniture and gigantic, painterly vases.

79 Barlby Road, W10 6AZ
Nearest station: Ladbroke Grove
ladbrokehall.com

50
MINT

A space for creative discovery

If you want to see the most electrifying design creatives working today, look no further: this space in Marylebone, led by talent-spotter extraordinaire Lina Kanafani, showcases a colourful array of ceramics, furniture, lighting and sculpture. There's beauty at every turn, with each piece handpicked by Kanafani who discovers, mentors and highlights unsung fresh talent from different design disciplines. The feeling on entering the gallery is that of stepping into a charming townhouse of an eclectic collector with the most imaginative taste. Think furniture made from discarded cardboard or woven from oversized textile bands, inflated aluminium chairs and interpretations of glassware and ceramics in the most unexpected shapes, colours and sizes.

3–5 Duke Street, W1U 3ED
Nearest station: Bond Street
mintgallery.co.uk

51
VITSŒ

Go-to shelving for design afficionados

Among the design-obsessed, the Vitsœ 606 Universal Shelving System is these days practically a badge of honour. Dreamt up in 1960 by German design legend Dieter Rams, its super-minimalist aesthetic and modular approach was built to grow as your life and requirements changed. In London, the best place to explore Rams' composed designs is the Vitsœ showroom in Marylebone, a very compact catalogue that includes the shelving, a set of nesting tables and an armchair that becomes a sofa. Minimalism exemplified.

21 Marylebone Lane, W1U 2NG
Nearest station: Bond Street
vitsoe.com

52
THE AUDLEY PUBLIC HOUSE

The art-flooded pub

A collaged ceiling by Phyllida Barlow, art and photography by Martin Creed, Andy Warhol and Don McCullin and a grand piano in the corner: this is more visual banquet than boozer. The Audley Public House in Mayfair had its glow-up courtesy of the minds behind world-renowned gallery Hauser & Wirth. While the ambiance inside retains the charm of a pub, with mahogany panelling and pints flowing, the artistic touches and small refurbishments (including the addition of an upside-down 19th-century clock) make it a seriously smart place for a beverage. There's lots more to discover on the upper floors, with Mount Street Restaurant continuing the gallery-worthy art displays and a special mosaic floor by Rashid Johnson.

41–43 Mount Street, W1K 2RX
Nearest station: Bond Street
theaudleypublichouse.com

… WEST

53
SARAH MYERSCOUGH GALLERY

Craftsmanship meets nature

It's easy to miss this gallery when you walk past it, tucked as it is behind Oxford Street and only accessible through a flight of steps. But you'll be glad you found it. Gallerist Sarah Myerscough has dedicated nearly three decades to discovering and championing the work of global artists operating at the cusp of art and craftsmanship, with a strong focus on wood but a full range that includes stoneware, plant fibres and flowers embedded in resin. Committed to amplifying the work of pioneering contemporary craftspeople in design, Myerscough's exhibitions are the best starting point to discover today's craft panorama. And they look fantastic, too: the honesty of the natural materials is evident in every piece, with organic forms abstracting the furniture's functionality.

34 North Row, W1K 6DH
Nearest station: Marble Arch
sarahmyerscough.com

54
PAUL SMITH NO 9 ALBEMARLE STREET

A playfully designed hideaway

Giving every outward appearance of being a typical Mayfair fashion store, on wandering inside visitors are treated to a wealth of surprising design. With splatterings of primary colours and stripes throughout, it is unmistakably 'Paul Smith'. Each area acts as a mini stage set for the clothes with whimsical features like dominoes decorating the walls and artworks from Paul's own archive, from contemporary artist Marc Quinn to 20th-century sculptor Alberto Giacometti. Don't miss the enormous multicoloured cactus that Smith designed with Italian brand Gufram as you stroll downstairs to the exhibition space that hosts an ever-revolving door of shows – all of them underpinned with that charming Paul Smith vibe.

9 Albemarle Street, W1S 4BL
Nearest station: Green Park
paulsmith.com

55
AESOP REGENT STREET

Multi-sensory refuge

Lose yourself in the clay-coloured interiors of Aesop's central London flagship, which is a noteworthy feast for the senses. Olfactory delights await in their 'Fragrance Armoire', relieving you of any stress you may be carrying after battling through busy Regent Street. The shop's design riffs off the neoclassical colonnades that adorn its exterior and mask a hidden retreat in the lower ground floor, where the lights are dimmed, and the colour scheme set a few shades deeper. There you'll find a treatment area set within deep wine-red walls and decorated with dark wooden furniture – all combined, you'll positively float out of your facial.

185 Regent Street, W1B 4JP
Nearest station: Piccadilly Circus
aesop.com

56
HEAL'S

Signature furniture in an iconic London store

If you visit just one furniture shop in London, it should be Heal's. Before stepping in, pause to appreciate its incredible facade, with a blue-tiled frieze dedicated to the art of making furniture: cabinetmakers, upholsterers, textile designers, bedding makers – they're all celebrated here by original emblems depicting their specialism. The expansive store occupies an entire block on Tottenham Court Road with an offering that includes all things home, from sofas by Ligne Roset and Muuto to iconic dining chairs by Knoll and Gubi, mesmerising lamps in transparent plastic by Kartell and coffee tables by the in-house brand, as well as accessories ranging from glassware to candles. If your budget is generous enough, this can really be the one-stop shop for furnishing your home.

196 Tottenham Court Road, W1T 7LQ
Nearest station: Goodge Street
heals.com

57
MARGARET HOWELL

Sartorial showcase with a twist

Fashion designer Margaret Howell embodies the quintessence of refined British style. More than just a showcase of her wares, Wigmore Street has as much an eye to design with the carefully selected products on view as it does to clothing. The weathered floors, wooden furniture, shop-long skylight and array of design books at the entrance make it a perfect destination when seeking design inspiration. Add in a host of rotating art exhibitions, tastefully curated Japanese tableware and the brand's own reissues of 20th-century furniture, and the result is one of the city's most surprising design hubs, fulfilling Howell's wish of it being 'more than just a retail space'.

34 Wigmore Street, W1U 2RS
Nearest station: Bond Street
margarethowell.co.uk

58
ANOTHER COUNTRY

Contemporary classics in natural materials

This furniture maker's motto is 'Designs for The Natural Home', and its offering is true to this mission. The all-wood, archetypal pieces nod to a classic style with a blink-and-you'll-miss-it contemporary twist, informed by Scandinavian and Japanese design. The furniture's simplicity goes hand in hand with the company's ethos of creating designs of enduring quality, made entirely from organic materials, manufactured responsibly and repaired throughout their life cycle by the company. Pop into the Marylebone shop for a full design service (everything is made to order) or to browse their offering in the serene space.

18 Crawford Street, W1H 1BT
Nearest station: Marylebone
anothercountry.com

IMAGE CREDITS

Intro section: Design Museum © Taran Wilkhu; Vitra © Taran Wilkhu; Present & Correct © Nick Dearden, courtesy of Architecture for London; St Giles Square © Ed Reeve; Another Country © Lesley Lau

Present & Correct © Nick Dearden, courtesy of Architecture for London; SCP: © Beth Evans, image courtesy SCP; Somerset House: © Ed Reeve, courtesy The London Design Biennale; Viaduct: © Viaduct Furniture Tokyo Bike: © Charlotte Schreiber; The Standard Hotel: © The Standard; Aram: first image © Ellen Christina Hancock, second image © Veerle Evans, third image © Ollie Tomlinson. All images courtesy Aram; Lee Broom Showroom: © Luke Hayes, image courtesy Lee Broom Showroom; magCulture: © Lesley Lau; Vitra Tramshed: © Taran Wilkhu Magma: © Ellen Christina Hancock; Tottenham Court Road Station: first image © Brian Harris / Alamy, second image © Francesco Montaguti St Giles Square: Swivel by Sabine Marcelis. Image © Ed Reeve; Twentytwentyone: © Lesley Lau; Isokon Gallery: © Tom de Gay, courtesy Isokon Gallery; Clay Station: © Rachael Smith; Young V&A: © David Parry, courtesy V&A; Flamboyance of Flamingos Playground: © Thierry Bal; A Bar With Shapes for a Name: ©Remy Savage; Jasper Morrison Shop: © Jasper Morrison Studio; Museum of the Home: © Em Fitzgerald for Museum of the Home; Ælfred: © Virginia Malavasi; The Marksman: © Tim George; Labour and Wait: © Lesley Lau; William Morris Gallery: © Charlotte Schreiber; Brunswick House: © Alexander Baxter, image courtesy Brunswick House; The Kiln Rooms: © Jessica Williams, image courtesy The Kiln Rooms; i you all: © Tian Khee Siong, courtesy of iyouall; Studio Voltaire: Artwork featured - Joanne Tatham & Tom O_Sullivan, The Institute For The Magical Effect Of Actually Giving A Shit (a note to our future self), 2021. A Studio Voltaire commission. Image courtesy of the Artists and The Modern Institute; Fashion and Textile Museum: © Robert Evans / Alamy Design District: © Taran Wilkhu; Cockpit: first image © James Winspear, second image © Carmen Gray; Bexleyheath High Streets for All: © We Made That /Antonia Carey/ London Borough of Bexley; V&A: © Peter Kelleher, images courtesy V&A; Cubitts Belgravia: © Nick Rees; Cromwell Place: © Cromwell Place; Sketch: © Ed Dabney; Design Museum: first image © Shruti Veermachineni / Gravity Road, second image © Hufton & Crow. Images courtesy Design Museum; The Conran Shop © The Conran Shop; Gallery FUMI © Tom Wright/ Penguins Egg Studio for Gallery FUMI; SoShiro © Nick Rochowski Photography, courtesy SoShiro Gallery; The Line: image © Angus Mills, Artwork © Rana Begum, Catching Colour, 2022; Modernity © James Harris for Modernity London; Shreeji Newsagents © Laura de Gunzberg for Gabriel Chipperfield; Japan House London first image © Lee Mawdsley, second image © Jeremie Souteyrat, third image © Zodee Media, The River Café © Modern House Liberty © Tania Volosianko; Ladbroke Hall © Mark Cocksedge, image courtesy Ladbroke Hall; Mint © Mint Gallery / Inge Clemente; Vitsœ © Vitsœ, image by Olivier Hess; The Audley © The Audley / Helen Cathcart; Sarah Myerscough Gallery: both images © Dan Fontanelli courtesy of Sarah Mysercough Gallery. Second image, installation view of 'The Nature of Things' exhibition at Sarah Myerscough Gallery; Paul Smith: image courtesy of Paul Smith; Aesop © Oskar Proctor, images courtesy Aesop Heals © chrispictures / Alamy; Margaret Howell © John Hooper Another Country © Lesley Lau

An Opinionated Guide to Design London
First edition

Published in 2024
by Hoxton Mini Press, London
Copyright © Hoxton Mini Press 2024.
All rights reserved.

Text by Sujata Burman
and Rosa Bertoli
Editing by Zoë Jellicoe
Design and production
by Richard Mason
Proofreading by Leona Crawford
Editorial support by Florence Ward

With thanks to Matthew Young for initial series design.

Please note: we recommend checking the websites listed for each entry before you visit for the latest information on price, opening times and pre-booking requirements.

The rights of Sujata Burman and Rosa Bertoli to be identified as the creator of this Work has been asserted under the Copyright, Designs and Patents Act 1988.

Thank you to all of the individuals and institutions who have provided images and arranged permissions. While every effort has been made to trace the present copyright holders we apologise in advance for any unintentional omission or error, and would be pleased to insert the appropriate acknowledgement in any subsequent edition.

No part of this publication may be reproduced, stored in a retrieval system, or transmitted in any form or by any means, electronic, mechanical, photocopying, recording or otherwise, without the prior written permission of the copyright owner.

A CIP catalogue record for this book is available from the British Library.

ISBN: 978-1-914314-70-4

Printed and bound by OZGraf, Poland

Hoxton Mini Press is an environmentally conscious publisher, committed to offsetting our carbon footprint. This book is 100 per cent carbon compensated, with offset purchased from Stand For Trees.

Every time you order from our website, we plant a tree:
www.hoxtonminipress.com

Selected opinionated guides in the series:

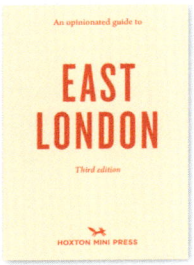

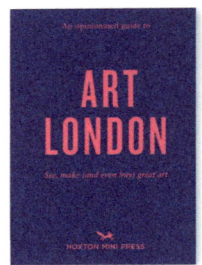

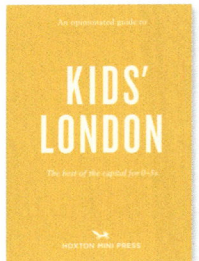

For more go to www.hoxtonminipress.com

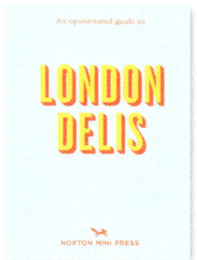

INDEX

A Bar with Shapes for a Name, 20
Ælfred, 23
Aesop Regent Street, 55
Another Country, 58
Aram Store, 7
The Audley Public House, 52
Bexleyheath High Streets for All, 35
Brunswick House, 28
Clay Station, 17
Coal Office, 14
Cockpit, 34
The Conran Shop, 41
Cromwell Place, 38
Cubitts Belgravia, 37
Design District, 33
Design Museum, 40
Fashion and Textile Museum, 32
Flamboyance of Flamingos, 19
Gallery FUMI, 42
Heal's, 56
iyouall, 30
Isokon Gallery, 16
Japan House London, 46
Jasper Morrison Shop, 21
The Kiln Rooms, 29
Labour and Wait, 25
Ladbroke Hall, 49
Lee Broom showroom, 8
Liberty, 48
The Line, 27
magCulture, 9
Magma, 11
Margaret Howell, 57
The Marksman, 24
Mint, 50
Modernity, 44
Museum of the Home, 22
Paul Smith No 9 Albemarle Street, 54
Present & Correct, 1
The River Cafe, 47
Sarah Myerscough Gallery, 53
SCP, 2
Shreeji Newsagents, 45
sketch, 39
Somerset House, 3
SoShiro, 43
St Giles Square, 13
The Standard, London, 6
Studio Voltaire, 31
tokyobike, 5
Tottenham Court Road Station, 12
twentytwentyone, 15
V&A, 36
Viaduct, 4
Vitra Tramshed, 10
Vitsœ, 51
William Morris Gallery, 26
Young V&A, 18